T0154245

THE LITTLE BOOK OF

Shit

BABY NAMES

Published by OH!
20 Mortimer Street
London W1T 3JW

ISBN 978-1-91161-050-2

Edited by: Malcolm Croft, Lesley Levene
Project manager: Russell Porter
Design: Tony Seddon
Production: Jess Arvidsson

A CIP catalogue record for this book is available from the British Library

Printed in Dubai

10 9 8 7 6 5 4 3 2 1

Jacket cover photograph: freepik.com

THE LITTLE BOOK OF
Shit
BABY NAMES

AND OTHER PEARLS OF PARENTING WISDOM

CONTENTS

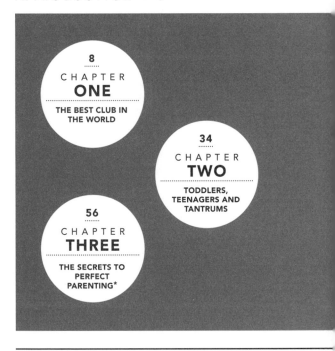
Just kidding. It's more jokes and stuff.

INTRODUCTION

Parenting is the world's *worst* best job. It is however also, paradoxically, the world's *best* worst job. Think about it. There's no company operating anywhere on this planet where employees not only work without pay but actually have to pay someone else (somwhere in the region of £150,000 up to the age of 18) so they can go to work.. There are no sick days or annual leave, the work is often unglamorous, degrading, physically debilitating, sticky, and smelly, with shifts that can last longer than 18 hours a day, for 365 days a year, with absolutely no benefits or job appreciation, or even acknowledgement that you're even doing the job to a decent standard. The kicker: you can't quit or retire. Yes, working for Family Inc., sucks big ones.

But, despite all this ball-breaking torture and misery, being a parent is also kind of neat. And, secretly, underneath all that resentment and disgust, and laundry, you really actually enjoy it. In fact, between you and me, at the end of the day, when peace and quiet floats through your abode like some heavenly freshly baked odour, you'll even admit that being a parent is probably the greatest thing you'll ever do, and that you love every second of the chaos. It's the best club of which you've ever been a member, you'll say.

It's in these moments of zen that you remember that the fun, awesome rock 'n' roller you were just a few years ago is dead. Good riddance.

Yep, parenthood is incredible, there's nothing else quite like it. And, if there is, you want no part of it.

To get you through the exhausting lows and the exhausting highs, we thought we'd compose this *Little Book of Shit Baby Names*, the best bedside companion for when you're wide awake at 6 a.m. waiting for a toddler to arise (or a teenager to arrive home) and the ideal antidote to all those other parenting manuals that preach from up on high about all the things you're doing wrong. There's no judgement here. OK, you might have called your baby boy Adele because it's the trendy thing to do. That's on you. Sure, you may have lost your two-year-old in the park earlier. They're speedy little buggers. So what if you let them play on the iPad for nine hours straight – they threatened to cut you if you took it away. Parenting isn't something that can be judged. There's too many moving parts. So, do what you like and do it however you feel like it. And, in the spirit of this carefree attitude, we created this tiny tome for your home, the perfect pick-me-up for when you realize that parenting isn't about raising beautiful children. It's a war. And one you must win.

Enjoy!

CHAPTER
ONE

You Know You're a Parent When

#1

You start to realize the irony
of the phrase
"sleeps like a baby".

Top Ten Baby Names: 2020

In the past decade or so, baby names have begun to increasingly move away from traditional and biblical names such as John, Joseph, Peter, Paul and Dave, etc. and once "normal" names like Ian, Norman, Nigel and Hubert have been pushed to the cringy fringes of likeability. So, at the start of 2020, these were the names that reigned supreme in the UK...

BOYS	GIRLS
Liam	Sophia
Jackson	Olivia
Noah	Emma
Aiden	Ava
Grayson	Aria
Caden	Isabella
Lucas	Amelia
Elijah	Mia
Oliver	Riley
Muhammed	Aaliyah

As seen on *goodhousekeeping.com*

Because We Say So:

#1

"A boy's best friend is his mother."

(Name the movie)

(*Psycho*, Alfred Hitchcock, 1960)

One Day You'll Thank Me:
PARENTAL ADVICE
#1

No matter how curious you find yourself, never ever lick a dark stain.

#1 Playlist
Fight Songs

Do you own a toddler and/or a teenager?
Next time they throw a tantrum or pick a fight
with you, consider your response and play the
appropriate track – really loud.

1. "You Can't Always Get What You Want" –
    The Rolling Stones
2. "We Can Work It Out" – The Beatles
3. "Comfortably Numb" – Pink Floyd
4. "Lord Protect My Child" – Bob Dylan
5. "We Take Care Of Our Own" – Bruce Springsteen
6. "All Shook Up" – Elvis Presley
7. "The Bitch Is Back" – Elton John
8. "Because One Of Us Was Wrong" – Porter
    Wagoner and Dolly Parton
9. "Children Go Where I Send Thee" – Johnny Cash
10. "Redemption Song" – Bob Marley

Swear Jar

While children swearing is a hilarious thing to see and hear, it is frowned upon in polite and civilized society. So, how do you continue your love of effin' and blindin' without inspiring and influencing your kids? Here's some nifty alternatives...

1. For fuck's sake – "Fox, owl, snake!"
2. Son of a bitch – "Son of a biscuit!"
3. Oh fuck – "Oh fudge!"
4. Oh shit – "Oh ships!"
5. Jesus Christ – "Cheese and rice!"
6. Fucking hell – "Fudging nell!"
7. Motherfucker – "Mother puffin!"
8. Fuck it – "Chuck it!"
9. Shut the fuck up – "Shut the front door!"
10. What the fuck – "What the frack!"

Dad Jokes

#1

Dad jokes are the worst. Buy yourself some peace and quiet and just start reciting and repeating these jokes ad nauseam. Your children will vacate your vicinity immediately.

1. Why should you not trust stairs?
   They're always up to something

2. What's black, white and read all over?
   A newspaper

3. What happened to the man with five legs?
   His trousers fitted him like a glove

Popular Baby Names: 2020

The following names were predicted to be the most popular baby names in the USA in 2020, as surveyed by motherly.com. To nobody's great surprise, these names are influenced by "high visibility celebrities or pop culture events" as well as a "fresh spin on a stylish sound or form."

GIRLS	BOYS
Adah	Austin
Reese	Alva
Mika	Acacius
Paisley	Tate
Amina	Diego
Teagan	Easton
Nova	Lucius
Aura	Cash
Pearl	Ash
Billie	Luca

As seen on motherly.com

Baby Names Around the World #1

Think outside the borders of your own nation and borrow the most popular baby names from other countries. These are the most trendy names at the moment.

England

GIRLS: Olivia, Amelia, Ava
BOYS: Oliver, George, Harry

France
GIRLS: Louise, Alice, Chloé
BOYS: Gabriel, Raphaël, Léon

Scotland
GIRLS: Olivia, Emily, Isla
BOYS: Jack, Oliver, James

Ireland
GIRLS: Emily, Grace, Emma
BOYS: Jack, James, Noah

Netherlands
GIRLS: Julia, Emma, Sophie
BOYS: Lucas, Levi, Finn

Germany
GIRLS: Emma, Mia, Hannah
BOYS: Ben, Paul, Leon

Shit Baby Name #1

Lear jet founder Bill Lear named his daughter – wait for it – Crystal Shanda Lear. Well, you would, wouldn't you?

Shit Baby Name Trend

#1

Reverse Baby Naming

Reverse baby naming started as a trend at the start of the new millennium according to several baby naming trend websites. By all accounts, these are the worst offenders. We'll let you reverse-engineer them.

Semaj	*Xela*
Adaj	*Lexa*
Siana	*Siri*
Nacirema	*Flor*
Nevar	*Yensid*
Traeh	*Adaven*

As seen on *babygaga.com*

Baby Naming
The Science

There is, of course, in these enlightened times, a "science" to baby naming. So, by following these simple rules, your child will be better than everyone else's in no time...

Give your baby a middle name (even an initial will do)

A study published in the *European Journal of Social Psychology* found that people using a middle initial are held in higher esteem, even if their name is Dick E. Bottom.

Give your son a Boy's name

Having a son? Don't give him a girly name. A study called "A Boy Named Sue" published in *Education Finance and Policy* revealed that boys with "feminine" names such as Ashley, Ainsley, Andy, Cameron, Jayden or Stevie can lead to those boys having "behavioural issues" later on in life.

Go prestigious

In a study carried out by Oxford University between 2008 and 2013, researchers found that certain names were more likely to attend the prestigious university than others. Peter, Simon and Anna were more likely than, say, Crystal, Travis and Koko.

Be appealing

Online daters with "appealing" names such as Charlotte and Spencer have much more success with the sex of their choice than those with names such as Nigel and Glenda. Sorry Glendas. People with "unattractive" names such as Brian and Paula are more likely to suffer from lower self-esteem.

Baby Naming
Checklist

As you would expect, there's a lot of basic nonsense online about HOW to choose a baby name. *Cosmopolitan* magazine probably summed it the most ridiculously. According to them, these are the five golden rules to baby naming...

1. Check what the name translates to in other languages.
2. Find out how popular it is (don't choose top ten).
3. Make sure it doesn't rhyme with anything awful.
4. Google the full name (check if the website exists, and if not buy it).
5. Sing "Happy Birthday' and insert the name (if it's awkward, ditch it).

As seen on *cosmopolitan.com*

Leg-ow!

There are, on average, approximately 75 plastic building bricks for every person on earth.

It is estimated that a parent will tread on approximately 143 pieces of brick in their parenting life,* causing them to scream blue bloody murder each and every single time. And there's a reason why these bricks are so fucking painful.

A single two-by-two brick can withstand up to 950 pounds of pressure. Because the Lego doesn't collapse when we step on it, it instead forces the pressure of your weight back up into your foot, causing immense pain. And the poor soles of our feet are incredibly sensitive: there are more than 200,000 sensory receptors all ready and waiting to receive pain.

*OK, we made this up. But the actual number is probably a lot higher.

You can learn many things from children. How much patience you have, for instance.

Franklin P. Adams

Mother's Motto
#1

Raising a strong child
requires a strong drink.

Icons of Parenting

#1

All Hail: Darth Vader

Darth Vader is perhaps the most famous put-upon parent in the galaxy. Think about it.

Like all fathers, Vader became evil at precisely the same time as his children were born – a day after a fairly horrific lava accident. Talk about a double whammy. He then spent the next 30 years keeping his twin children at a safe distance from a megalomaniacal emperor, only for his idiot son, Luke, deciding to travel halfway across the galaxy to find Vader, hellbent on confronting him and vowing his destruction, despite Vader offering Luke a rather tempting offer to work with him as co-ruler of the galaxy, which was rudely rejected by Luke.

After reverting to the light side of the Force, as his son demanded, Vader then *died* while trying to save his son's life. Luke then burned Vader's body on an open flame. All in the same day. While all of this father-son bonding was happening, Vader's daughter, Leia, remained nonplussed by his absence and never called him once to say hello.

To add insult to injury, he was given the moniker Darth Vader, German for "Dark Father", even though all he ever wanted was to *not* be a father.

CHAPTER
TWO

TODDLERS,
TEENAGERS AND
TANTRUMS

Know it All

Rather frustratingly, children ask their parents a staggering 73 questions every day, half of which parents struggle to answer correctly, according to a recent study reported in the *Independent*. Let's sort this out once and for all...

1. **Why do people die?**
   Because they get ill from answering too many questions.

2. **Where did I come from?**
   Go ask your mother.

3. **What is God?**
   You better ask them.

4. **Is Santa Real?**
   If you want him to be, he is. However, remember, Mummy and Daddy buy the presents for Santa to deliver. So, consider him more like a daily postman than a magical deity.

5. **How was I made?**

   Unintentionally.

6. **What does "We can't afford it" mean?**

   *Every night a monster called TaxMan steals
   lots of Mummy and Daddy's money from under
   our bed and that's why we can't afford to buy
   you a new bike.*

7. **Why do I have to go to school?**

   Because I have to go to work.

8. **When you die who will I live with?**

   I don't care. I'll be dead.

9. **Why is the sky blue?**

   It's the colour of God's wee. Ask God about it.

10. **Why can't I stay up as late as you?**

    *You don't. I'm asleep two minutes after
    you are.*

As seen on *independent.co.uk*

Dad Bods
(and how to get the perfect one)

"Dad bods" are revered in the health and fitness communities for being prime examples of where power and body mass meet in, and around, the middle. Dad bods are the peak of physical male fitness and consistently found incredibly alluring and sexy by their female counterparts.

Disregard the five-second rule: Any food on the floor is automatically yours.

1. Waste not want not – any leftovers are fair game.
2. Never say never to birthday party cakes.
3. Stress eating is not only allowed, it's mandatory.
4. Partners prefer you rounder because:
   (a) you're less likely to have an affair
   (b) you remind them of their fathers.
5. A beer belly is not fat – that's pure power.

Bedside Companion

#1

Are you wired and awake after running around keeping those mini versions of yourself alive? If so, these brain-boggling statistics and useless facts will help you drift off to sleep in seconds.

1. A jiffy is the actual amount of time it takes light to travel a distance of one centimetre – about 33.3564 picoseconds.

2. The line between the two numbers in a fraction is called the vinculum.

3. In chess, after both players move, there are 400 possible board moves. After the second pair of turns, there are 197,742 possible moves, and after three moves, 121 million.

4. The names of each continent ends with the same letter it starts with. Try it!

5. A pig's orgasm can last for 30 minutes. Picture it.

6. A whale's penis is called a dork.

Father's Figures
#1

50 per cent of all new dads put on as much as 30 pounds during their partners' pregnancies.

Slanguage Barrier

The invention of the smartphone has caused nothing but headaches for parents of teenagers. Parents must remain vigilant of pre-adolescent "slanguage", or at the very least, use it to look cool in front of their kids. Here's the best of a bad bunch.

Wavey – drunk or high
Zerg – to gang up on someone
Swipe right – to like
Nang/nanging – excellent
What's good – hello
Peng – attractive

Long – boring
Moist – awful
Turnt – crazy
Smash – sex
Tweeking – worried
Hella lit – really cool
Af – as fuck
Goat – awesome (greatest of all time)
Shook – amazed
Savage – cruel
Woke – knowledgeable
Shade – insult
Gucci – cool
Fire – very good
Choice – the best
Idek – I don't even know
Fleek – supercool

*Relevant as of March 2020 (yep, already out of date)

Pretentious Parenting Platitudes #1

The one thing that irks parents the most is when other people try to parent their kids or tell them how to do parenting properly. So, here's a list of overused parenting quotes that are written by clever people who think they know better than you. Feel free to flip your finger at them because, as you know, it's all bullshit.

"The most important thing that parents can teach their children is how to get along without them."

Frank A. Clark

"*Fathering is not something perfect men do, but something that perfects the man. The end product of child-raising is not the child but the parent.*"

    Frank Pittman

"*Being a mother is an attitude, not a biological relation.*"

    Robert A. Heinlein

"*There are times as a parent when you realize that your job is not to be the parent you always imagined you'd be, the parent you always wished you had. Your job is to be the parent your child needs, given the particulars of his or her own life and nature.*"

    Ayelet Waldma

"*The value of marriage is not that adults produce children, but that children produce adults.*"

    Peter De Vries

"It's not only children who grow. Parents do too. As much as we watch to see what our children do with their lives, they are watching us to see what we do with ours. I can't tell my children to reach for the sun. All I can do is reach for it, myself."

Joyce Maynard

"There are two lasting bequests we can give our children. One is roots. The other is wings."

Hodding Carter, Jr.

"Children have never been very good at listening to their elders, but they have never failed to imitate them."

James Baldwin

"Don't worry that children never listen to you; worry that they are always watching you."

Robert Fulghum

"Your children will become what you are; so be what you want them to be."

David Bly

"My father didn't tell me how to live, he lived, and let me watch him do it."

Clarence Budinton Kelland

"Children are educated by what the grown-up is and not by his talk."

Carl Jung

"It is easier to build strong children than to repair broken men."

Frederick Douglass

"Do not handicap your children by making their lives easy."

Robert A Heinlein

Hot Gossip

You may be surprised to learn that the phrase "Netflix and chill" does not mean what it actually says. The phrase is, indeed, code for sex, and used predominantly by teenagers.

So, next time you tell your children you're "Netflix and chilling" expect an all-round and resounding "Bleurgh" to emanate from their mouths.

Awkward Baby Names

These babies have actually existed. Can you imagine how hard their teenage years were?

Dick Bellringer
Mike Litoris
Shawn Dickensheets
Jack Goff
BJ Cobbledick
Christian Guy
Willie Stroker
Ben Dover
Rusty Kuntz
Agusta Wind

Anice Bottom
Barbie Cue
Don Key
Etta Lott
Fay King
Gladys Friday
Justin Case
Paige Turner
Tim Burr
Rob Berry

Baby Name Comebacks: 2020

Hey you! Yes, you! You look like you haven't got the foggiest what to call your new sprog. Don't panic! Just choose one of this apparently "on trend" naming themes that will make you and your child seem "ahead of the edge".

Trend #1: Cute names for boys, e.g. Archie, Alfie, Charlie

Trend #2: Girls' names ending in "lyn", e.g. Evelyn, Roselyn, Caitlyn

Trend #3: Girls' names ending in "a", e.g. Greta, Tessa, Martha, Cara

Trend #4: Short names for boys, e.g. Kit, Eli, Kai

Trend #5: Old-lady names for girls, e.g. Scarlett, Gertrude, Maude

Trend #6: Ethnic names, e.g. Mohammed (Mo), Khaled (Kal), Ahmed

Trend #7: Unisex girls' names, e.g. Billie, Riley, Quinn, Sawyer

Trend #8: Boys' names ending in "s", e.g. Miles, Lucas, Luis, Elias

Trend #9: Cosmos-inspired names, e.g. Luna, Cosmo, Phoenix, Rocket

Trend #10: Short names for girls, e.g. Mia, Sia, Zoe

Songspiration: The Beatles

Taking inspiration for baby names from song titles is only acceptable if the songs are by The Beatles. Thankfully, there's lots (too many?) to choose from. These, and only these, have our seal of approval.

"Penny Lane"
"Julia"
"Martha, My Dear"
"Dear Prudence"
"Eleanor Rigby"
"Lucy in the Sky with Diamonds"
"Hey Jude"
"Rocky Raccoon"
"Lovely Rita"
"Maggie Mae"

"Maxwell's Silver Hammer"
"Polythene Pam"
"Sexy Sadie"
"Doctor Robert"
"Michelle"
"Dizzy Miss Lizzy"
"Lady Madonna"
"The Continuing Story of Bungalow Bill"
"What's the New Mary Jane"
"Anna (Go to Him)"

"Foreign" Baby Names

Nothing screams how cool and liberal (and smug) you are than calling you're white middle-class baby a name that sounds, well, anything but a white middle-class baby. Even though they're very similar to their English equivalent, these will make you the envy of every playgroup and nursery...

Alejandra
Chiara
Delphine
Elodie
Fabienne
Gioia (pronounced Joy)
Inez
Jocasta
Kalindi
Larisa

Maeve
Natalya
Oriana
Paloma
Quintana
Solange
Tamar
Viveca
Xanthe
Zusanna

Hilarious Things New Parents Do

We've all made these "mistakes", but that doesn't mean we can't laugh at them.

1. Change a nappy when it's dry (just because you feel like you should).

2. Admired the size of your child's BM (this never loses its magic).

3. Taken your baby to A&E for something ridiculously trivial (and then felt embarrassed for being there).

4. Finished the remains of baby food (waste not want not).

5. Mutter "That'll do" when trying for two hours to fit a car seat for the first time (you're still unsure if it's setup correctly).

6. Smuggled an old Babygro to work just so you could smell your baby while at work.

7. Punched and kicked any enthusiastic dog that tried to get too close to your baby at the park (beware of the parent).

8. Fallen asleep in places not usually reserved for sleeping (top of the stairs, on the toilet, etc.).

9. Played keepie-uppie with a really wet and heavy nappy (just to see how many you could do).

10. Stared at the baby monitor until you see your baby's chest go up and down (you never stop doing this).

CHAPTER
THREE

THE SECRETS TO PERFECT PARENTING*

Just kidding. It's more jokes and stuff.

Drinking Games

While these games are not recommended, practical, or even safe, they are fun. If you want to introduce a bit more chaos into your parenting, then these drinking games are a good starter for ten. Drink a shot of liquor every time your child does one of the following…

1. Screams directly into your ear.

2. Kicks you in the nuts.

3. Pisses everywhere but down the toilet.

4. Sleeps horizontally in your bed.

5. Poops as soon as you've changed a nappy.

6. Pushes an entire plate of food on the floor.

7. Slamms their bedroom door shut.

8. Refuses to acknowledge your existence OR won't stop bothering you.

9. Poops in the bathtub and tries to pick it up.

10. Throws itself down on the floor and kicks and screams in an apoplectic rage.

Cocktail Recipes
#1

Why not try one of our signature cocktail recipes, tailor-made for your parenting moods...

#1: Deep Sleep

It's 7 p.m. The baby's down for the night. You've got 12 hours to party. Celebrate with the 12-hour blues. It'll have you in bed, lights out, by 7.30 p.m.

- Three shots of whisky
- Two tablespoons of hot chocolate powder
- A splash of double cream
- Hot water

Mix the whisky and chocolate powder in a mug. Top up with hot water and mix well. Add a big splash of double cream to really slow the senses. Drink slowly, preferably in bed.

Reasons You Love Your Kids

**It's always handy to have this written down
somewhere for when you forget...**

1. That giggle they make when tickled.

2. Knowing only you can kiss it better when they're hurt.

3. That feeling when they want to hold your hand.

4. The first time they say "Mummy" or "Daddy" and know that it means you.

5. That feeling you get from knowing you'll do anything for their happiness.

6. That sparkle in their eyes that informs you they're about to cause trouble.

7. That moment you realize that they're smarter now than you've ever been.

8. That feeling you get when you know they're safe.

9. The strength that you draw from their unconditional love (pre-teen).

10. Oh, and because one day it'll be their turn to support you.

Parent Bingo

Being a parent means doing the same thing over and over, day in day out, and following routines. To ensure that your day doesn't become too stale, introduce a bit of Parent Bingo into your and your partner's day. First one to tick off all these items in one day – wins!

1. Gets dressed all by themselves.

2. Says "I love you" (and seems to not want anything in return).

3. All vegetables eaten without moaning.

4. Sits quietly for up to ten minutes.

5. Doing something upon being asked the first time to do it.

6. Gets bored of playing with their iPad and reads a book.

7. Takes themselves to bed.

8. Doesn't pit Mummy and Daddy against one another.

9. Shows appreciation for all that they have.

10. Sleeps the whole night without getting into your bed.

Top Ten Baby Names: 2025

Baby names of the future can be predicted by the famous people of today and the next few years. In this new Golden Age of Staring at A Screen, parents are increasingly choosing their baby names from popular, but fictional – and often highly ridiculous – TV, movie, app and literary characters. Expect to hear more of these names coming soon to a playgroup near you.

BOYS	GIRLS
Kylo	*Rey*
Archie	*Meghan*
Logan	*Eleven*
Kit	*Jett*
Poe	*Sansa*
Tony	*Khalessi*
Tyrion	*Arya*
Kal-El	*Cersei*
Thor	*Zori*
Benedict	*Wanda*

Baby Talk
#1

For parents, every day starts exactly the same: with the exhausted uttering of these famous first five phrases:

1. Eugh.
2. Not this again.
3. It's your turn.
4. But I did it yesterday.
5. I need ten more minutes.

Date Night

Just when you thought it was safe to dip your toes back in the late-night world of socializing with your friends – or, worse, a date night – after years lost in the sleep-deprived newborn wilderness, you are faced with babysitters – the best racket in town. Here are the average Date Night costs. If these numbers don't make you and your partner want to jump back under the covers and make another baby, nothing will. And they say love don't cost a thing...

Babysitting Rate, London: £12 an hour, approx. five hours: £60

Taxi: £20, return

Dinner: £45 per person, including alcohol

Cinema: £15 per person, excluding drinks/treats

Taxi for Babysitter: £15

Total Cost: £215

Worth It: For one fucking night out with a person you're already married to – NO!

66

A two-year-old is kind of like
having a blender, but you
don't have a top for it.

99

Jerry Seinfeld

Guess What

Sugar does not make kids go all loopy and hyper. Any food that affects blood-sugar levels, be it a tomato, banana or a chocolate bar, can create an adrenalin surge.

If you child locates their inner speed demon, bring them back down to normal speed with a treat pumped full of fibre – popcorn, cereal, nuts, rice.

Reasons You Love Your Kids

For that precious sleepy-cuddly cute moment just after they've woken up. For that brief insta-second when they aren't kicking you in the balls, or throwing their faeces on the floor, or having a meltdown because you turned off the 27th episode of *Peppa Pig*. That moment makes it all worthwhile. Right?

Top Ten Lies You Tell Your Children

#1

If you eat all your vegetables, your body will turn them into chocolate.

One Day You'll Thank Me:
PaReNTal ADvice
#2

Never teach your child
to whistle.

#2 Playlist
Explicit Lyrics

Had enough of your children but also still legally responsible for them? While it's best not to drop F, C, or S-bombs yourself why not tell your children what you really think of them subconsciously through these songs. "Hey, Siri, play..."

1. "Killing in the Name of" – Rage Against the Machine:
2. "Fuck You" – Cee Lo Green
3. "Shut The Fuck Up" – Backyard Babies
4. "One Step Closer" – Linkin Park
5. "I Hate You So Much Right Now" – Kelis
6. "The Way I Am" – Eminem
7. "Breaking Dishes" – Rihanna
8. "I'm Not Your Mother, I'm Not Your Bitch" – Courtney Barnett
9. "Bad Day" – Daniel Powter
10. "IDGAF" – Dua Lipa

Playground Fact

Why do ABCD, Twinkle Twinkle and Baa Baa Black Sheep all have the same melody?*

* The melodies are the same as they are all variations of a 1761 melody called, 'Ah vous dirais-je, Maman' by French composer Bouin.

Reasons You Love Your Kids

#3

When you lament that "they grow up so fast" and then your realize that one day you might actually get your life back.

Top Ten Lies
You Tell Your Children
#2

Sitting too close to the TV will ruin your eyesight.*

*Children are actually better at focusing on up-close objects than adults.

#3 Playlist
Baby Love Songs

When your children are playing and behaving like superstars, show them how much you love them with these super sappy cheesy love songs.

1. "(Everything I Do) I Do It for You" – Bryan Adams
2. "I Want to Know What Love Is" – Foreigner
3. "Sugar, Sugar" – The Archies
4. "You Were Meant for Me" – Jewel
5. "She Will Be Loved" – Maroon 5
6. "You Are So Beautiful" – Joe Cocker
7. "Can You Feel the Love Tonight" – Elton John
8. "More Than Words" – Extreme
9. "I Just Called to Say I Love You" – Stevie Wonder
10. "You're Beautiful" – James Blunt

One Day You'll Thank Me:
Parental Advice
#3

Turn the dull or chaotic events of your day at work into a riveting bedtime story, full of heroes (you), monsters (your boss) and princes and princesses (your office crushes).

MoTHeR'S MoTTo
#2

You do not negotiate with terrorists.

Father's Figures

#2

60 per cent of a parent's daily calories come from leftovers (and licking knives).

Dad Jokes
#2

More dad jokes to help send your children on their merry little way away from you. (Pretending to fart also helps.)

1. Two cannibals are eating a clown. One says to the other: "Does this taste funny to you?"

2. Three fish are in a tank. One fish asks the others, "How do you drive this thing?"

3. What do you call a pony with a cough?
   A little hoarse

Top Unisex Names: 2020

Gender-neutral baby names are more popular now than ever. Nameberry.com predicted these names to be bigger than Jesus in the USA in 2020. So, get in now, before they become old hat.

Ellis
Phoenix
Remi /Remy
Marlowe
Shea
Zephyr
Darcy
Rowan
Quinn
Emerson

Shit Baby Name #2

Bob

//bu·hb//

Some names deserve to die. Prime example number one: Bob. It's more of an annoying sound, a noise made by a car going over a bumpy road, than a name. As an ironic girl's name, it's the worst. For boys, it's just plain stupid. Imagine a newborn, cherubic-looking baby... called Bob. Ridiculous.

Bob began as a variation on Rob, short for Robert, sometime in the Middle Ages when rhyming names became all the rage: Richard became Rick, Hick, or Dick; William became Will, Gill, or Bill; and Robert became Rob, Hob, Dob, Nob, or Bob.

I like you young Bob. You've got balls. **"**

Lord Percy, *Blackadder*

Famous Bobs:

Bob Dylan, Bob Marley, Bob Ross, Bob Saget, Bob Hope, Bob Geldof, Bob Hoskins.

There were 5,963 Roberts born in the UK in 2019. That's potentially a lot of Bobs you need to go out of your way to avoid.

Bob has a rating of ONE like out of TEN.

Baby Names Around the World
#2

The world's most popular names, as of 2019.

Sweden
GIRLS: Alice, Maja, Lilly
BOYS: William, Liam, Noah

Spain
GIRLS: Lucia, Sofia, María
BOYS: Lucas, Hugo, Martín

Iceland
GIRLS: Emiía, Emma, Elísabet
BOYS: Alexander, Aron, Mikael

New Zealand
GIRLS: Charlotte, Isla, Olivia
BOYS: Oliver, Jack, Noah

Australia
GIRLS: Charlotte, Olivia, Ava
BOYS: Oliver, William, Jack

Portugal
GIRLS: Maria, Matilde, Leonor
BOYS: João, Rodrigo, Francisco

Norway
GIRLS: Emma, Nora, Olivia
BOYS: Lucas, Filip, Oliver

Italy
GIRLS: Sofia, Guilia, Aurora
BOYS: Francesco, Leonardo, Alessandro

CHAPTER
FOUR

WOULD A ROSE BY
ANY OTHER
NAME

SMELL AS SWEET?

Shit Baby Name

#3

Jermaine Jackson, of legendary
Jackson 5 fame, and wife
Hazel Joy Gordy, daughter of
legendary Motown producer Berry
Gordy, called their son – wait for it –
Jermajesty Jermaine Jackson.

Shit Baby Name Trend

#2

The QWERTY Effect

According to babygaga.com, a new study has shown that more and more parents are choosing their baby names based on the "QWERTY Effect", a phenomenon that shows a preference to use letters typed on the right side of a keyboard. Hence the reason why names such as Olivia, Liam, Noah, Violet, Fred, Drew and Sarah remain in the Top Ten of most QWERTY-using nations.

Celebrity
Baby Names

People, even annoying celebrities, can call their children whatever they want. And, lord knows, we don't need any more Dave's in the world. But, come on…. it's getting ridiculous, right?

Tom Fletcher and Giovanna Fletcher's son –
Buzz Michelangelo

Penn Jillette and Emily Zoltan's daughter –
Moxie Crimefighter

Cardi B and Offset's son – Kulture Kiari Cepheus

Kylie Jenner and Travis Scott's daughter – Stormi

Kim Kardashian and Kanye West's children in general –
Psalm, Saint, Chicago, North

Gwyneth Paltrow and Chris Martin's daughter – Apple

Katie Price and Peter Andre's daughter – Princess Tiaamii

Paula Yates and Michael Hutchence daughter –
    Heavenly Hiraani Tiger Lily

Woody Allen and Mia Farrow's son – Satchel

Julia Stiles and Preston J. Cook's son – Strummer

Beyonce and Jay-Z's son – Sir

Lucky Blue Smith and Stormi Lee's daughter – Gravity

Bradley Cooper and Irina Shayk's daughter – Lea de Seine

Rob Kardashian and Blac Chyna's daughter – Dream

Jamie and Jools Oliver's son – River Rocket

Megan Fox and Brian Austin Green's son –Journey River

Alanis Morrisette and Mario Treadway's daughter –
    Onyx Solace

Gwen Stefani and Gavin Rossdale's son – Apollo Bowie

Ok, that's enough.

Baby Names: Lost in Translation

Before you get your baby naming book out, just quickly check off these names – it may save you a lot of ridicule if you ever decided to take your little one travelling...

Argentina
Pete = blowjob

Japan
Gary = diarrhoea

Netherlands
Dom = stupid
Bill = arse

Denmark
Tessa = to piss

France
Nick = fuck
Mallory = unfortunate

Norway
Mark = worm

Germany
Chloe = toilet
Todd = death

Italy
Pippa = masturbation / handjob

Greece
Lisa = rabies
Camila = camel

Russia
Amanda = female genital
Luke = manhole

"

No matter how much time
you spend reading books
or following your intuition,
you're gonna screw it up.
Fifty times. You can't do
parenting right.

"

Alan Arkin

I don't know what's more exhausting about parenting: the getting up early, or acting like you know what you're doing.

Jim Gaffigan

Mother-in-Law Fun

Next time you play Scrabble with your mother-in-law throw these words in for fun using some of the letters from 'mother-in-law':

1. Timeworn
2. Antihero
3. Wartime
4. Moaner
5. Loather

Anagrams of the word "mother-in-law" include:

1. Woman Hitler
2. Minor Wealth
3. Wraith Melon

Mother's Motto
#3

Silence is golden. Unless
you have kids.
Then it's suspicious.

Icons of Parenting

#2

All Hail: Homer Simpson

Homer Simpson's rise to perhaps becoming the greatest father that never lived – he's a cartoon, remember – is as telling about fathers as it is hilarious. Homer is the beacon for modern dads all around the world; he is their voice and their most significant role model. Never has a father loved his children so unconditionally, and yet been so indifferent to raising them properly. Homer's simple childlike mind often meant that his children were more his peers than his kin. To celebrate this wonderful dad, here are his ten best parenting tips:

1. "Kids, you tried your best and you failed miserably. The lesson is, never try."

2. "Marriage is like a coffin, and each kid is another nail."

3. "I think the saddest day of my life was when I realized I could beat my dad at most things, and Bart experienced that at the age of four."

4. "Kids are the best. You can teach them to hate the things you hate. And they practically raise themselves, what with the internet and all."

5. "The key to parenting is don't overthink it. Because overthinking leads to... what were you talking about?"

6. "Just because I don't care doesn't mean I don't understand."

7. "Son, if you really want something in this life, you have to work for it. Now quiet! They're about to announce the lottery numbers."

8. "Marge, don't discourage the boy! Weaselling out of things is important to learn. It's what separates us from the animals! Except the weasel."

9. "When I look at the smiles on all the children's faces, I just know they're about to jab me with something."

10. "It's not easy to juggle a pregnant wife and a troubled child, but somehow I managed to fit in eight hours of TV a day."

You Know You're a Parent When #2

You have to talk a toddler down from the edge when you tell them it's ridiculous to take an umbrella out on a hot sunny summer's day.

Dad Bods

Good news for new dads – you're not fat. You're just another victim of the merciless Couvade syndrome. Best. Excuse. Ever. But what is it, you ask?

For centuries it has been observed that new and expecting fathers "suffer" from sympathetic pregnancy pains. It is known as the "pregnant dad" or Couvade syndrome. These are the symptoms: indigestion, weight gain, fatigue, food cravings, vomiting, diarrhoea, constipation, nausea, mood swings, stomach pain, bloating, cramping, headache, backache, toothache. So, basically, how you feel most of the time, or hungover.

Guess What

#1

Can you name any animated
or cartoon films where both
parents (or grandparents) are
present and don't die during
the movie? What are these film
producers and film makers trying
to say – kids are better off with
dead parents?

Father's Figures
#3

A dad eats, on average,
400 more calories
a day than a non-parent man.

Bedside Companion

#2

Are you in bed at 7.30 p.m. Don't worry, you'll be soon enough. Until then, help yourself fall asleep with these nuggets of non-interest.

1. There is approximately one chicken for every human being in the world.

2. Ants stretch and yawn every morning before starting their day.

3. The pop you hear when you crack your knuckles is actually a bubble of gas burning.

4. The thumbnail grows the slowest, the middle nail the fastest, nearly four times faster than toenails.

5. In the last 3,500 years, there have been approximately 230 years of peace throughout the civilized world.

6. The length of beard an average man would grow if he never shaved is 8.38 metres ($27^1/2$ feet).

7. $111,111,111 \times 111,111,111 = 12,345,678,987,654,321$.

Extinct Baby Names

In the good ol' days, i.e. the 1950s, the most boring (read: traditional) baby names were considered the best. That ain't true today. The following baby boy names stand on the edge of existence in 2019, according to a recent study. And quite rightly. They're dull as shit. Good riddance...

BOYS	GIRLS
Neville	*Doris*
Malcolm	*Paula*
Clarence	*Wendy*
Derek	*Elaine*
Geoffrey	*Sharon*
Wayne	*Sally*
Gary	*Kirsty*
Neil	*Chelsea*
Nigel	*Rachel*
Barry	*Jordan*

As seen in *The Sun/Mother&Baby/Cosmopolitan*

Reasons You Love Your Kids
#4

When your child farts and it
makes them laugh.

Top Ten Lies
You Tell Your Children
#3

Bunny has gone to live with
another family because you were
too much of a naughty little boy.
(It's dead.)

One Day You'll Thank Me:
Parental Advice
#4

Tell your children every day WHY you love them, not how much. Ask them to do the same about you. Then exploit these weaknesses by withholding them.

Reasons You Love Your Kids

#5

When you realize they take after you more than your partner.

#4 Playlist
Car Journeys*

Anything to stop them from whinging all the way...

1. "The Alphabet Song"
2. "This Old Man"
3. "She'll Be Coming Round the Mountain"
4. "Six Little Ducks"
5. "The Ants Go Marching"
6. "You Are My Sunshine"
7. "If You're Happy and You Know It"
8. "Row, Row, Row Your Boat"
9. "Old MacDonald Had a Farm"
10. "The Wheels on the Bus"

*In fact, we dare you to sing all these in order from start to finish and then measure how much sanity you have left in your body.

One Day You'll Thank Me:
Parental Advice
#5

At the weekends, give your children a wrapped present box that's empty inside. Tell them that what's inside is "whatever you want it to be".
That'll buy you 20 minutes of distraction.

Reasons You Love Your Kids

#6

When you get the opportunity to embarrass them, you go nuclear.

Top Ten Lies
You Tell Your Children
#4

The star symbol on your iPhone
connects straight to Santa.
If activated, he'll know
you've been a naughty child.

One Day You'll Thank Me:
Parental Advice
#6

Keep a large jar full of coins. Every time your child behaves give them a coin to put in their own jar. When the jar is full, they can spend the money on whatever they want.*

* When they're not looking take back just enough coins so the jar never quite fills up.

Dad Jokes
#3

Still pestered by pesky kids?
Drop these joke bombs and watch the room clear...

1. What did the egg do for fun?
    Karaoke

2. You know what the loudest pet you can get is?
    A trumpet

3. What goes down but doesn't come up?
    A yo

Popular Dog Names

Just because Indiana Jones was named after the dog doesn't mean that you should do the same with the fruit of your loins. These are the most popular dog names in the UK. So, stay away from them...

1. Bella
2. Poppy
3. Alfie
4. Lola
5. Max

6. Charlie
7. Luna
8. Bailey
9. Teddy
10. Buddy

As seen on *standard.co.uk*

ShiT BaBy Names
#4

Iconic (if nonconformist) American musician Frank Zappa spared his children from dull, traditional names. If anything, like his music, he went a little too far.

Diva Thin Muffin Zappa (daughter)
Moon Unit Zappa (daughter)
Dweezil Zappa (son)

CHAPTER
FIVE

KIDS OF ALL
AGES

Shit Baby Name Trend

#3

Gender Stereotyping

Even today, approaching the third decade of the twenty-first century, gender stereotyping remains omnipresent. Parents still want their sons to have big boy names and daughters to have cute little petite names.

This stereotyping is achieved by the placement of the vowels A and O. They create "large-sounding" boy names such as James, John, Jack, Joel, Dave, Don, Dan, Martin.

For girls, the placement of the vowels I and E, which create "small" sounding girly names like Emily, Angie, Chloe, Sophie, Phoebe, Zoe, etc.

When your children are
teenagers, it's important to
have a dog so that someone
in the house is happy to
see you.

Nora Ephron

Dad Jokes
#4

"

Kids are maturing so much earlier now. Every Sunday I've been taking my six-year-old over to the park to play on the swings and the slides. Last Sunday he refused to go. He said he's too old for that sort of thing. So now I'll have to play on the swings on my own.

"

Les Dawson

Mother's Motto
#4

Dogs can smell cancer.
Kids can smell parents
relaxing.

Icons of Parenting

#3

All Hail: Queen Gertrude

"The lady doth protest too much, methinks."
Queen Gertrude in *Hamlet*, Act 3, Scene 2,
William Shakespeare

William Shakespeare sure knew how to write about parenting and make it seem true to life. Take Hamlet's mother, Queen Gertrude, for example. She married Hamlet's uncle, Claudius, almost immediately after Hamlet's father death (rather suspiciously, as it turned out). Gertrude wasn't fussed about her husband's death, nor did she give a damn about her son's feelings about either his father's dead or her remarriage, or any aspect of his life. But then, she probably thought Hamlet loved their relationship enough for the both of them. Anyway, Gertrude died a misunderstood mother: all she wanted was to stay the queen of her nice big home and her bloody overdramatic son got in the way.

Guess What

#2

A pregnant goldfish
is called a twit.

Fussy Eaters

If your children are fussy vegetable eaters tell them that cruciferous vegetables such as cauliflower, cabbage, kale, garden cress, bok choy, broccoli, Brussels sprouts and similar green leafy vegetables contain raffinose – an indigestible sugar that methane-producing bacteria in the colon feed on and release gas in the process.

They also contain sulphur so the smell is really bad. Ironically, the healthier the food you eat, the worse your farts will smell – if that doesn't entice them to eat healthy, nothing will.

Cocktail Recipes
#2

Why not try one of our signature cocktail recipes, tailor-made for your parenting moods...

#2: Wake Up Call

It's 5 a.m. Your baby is stirring. Get ready for chaos with this zingy and zesty little number.

- One shot of vodka
- One glass of orange juice
- One raw egg
- One teaspoon of paprika
- One teaspoon of coffee powder

Drown the vodka in orange juice, crack in the raw egg and sprinkle in the paprika and coffee powder. If this doesn't wake you up, your baby will.

Winning Lottery Numbers

Being a parent costs much more than an arm and a leg – it steals from your soul too. However, we know a guy who knows a guy who went out with a girl who works for the National Lottery and apparently the following sets of numbers are all 'guaranteed' to win big this year.*
What have you got to lose?

11	17	22	36	41	8
3	09	12	18	19	1
15	28	33	34	45	12
4	16	29	47	56	22

By the way, the six most commonly drawn balls on the National Lottery since its inception in 1994 are: 23, 38, 31, 25, 33 and 11.

*By playing these numbers you legally agree to share 50 per cent of all earnings with the publisher of this book.

You Know You're a Parent When #3

You're scared to sit down and get comfortable because you know it'll only be a matter of seconds before all hell breaks loose.

Parenting Clichés

(You Never Thought You'd Actually Say)

In the world before children, you and your partner probably believed that you would be a different type of parent and raise your children differently from how your parents did. How's that going? These are the phrases you grew up with – and now, I bet all the money in your pockets, you use them too…

"If you want to act like a child, I'll treat you like one."

"Quieten down, I can't even hear myself think."

"If you keep making that face, it'll freeze that way."

"One day you'll thank me."

"Because I said so, that's why!"

"As long as you're under my roof, you live by my rules."

"Ask a stupid question, get a stupid answer."

"If all of your friends jumped off a bridge, would you?"

"Talking to you is like talking to a brick wall."

"You better wipe that look off your face."

"Don't make me: tell you again/come back there/turn this car around et al."

As seen on huffpost.com

Alternative Nursery Rhymes #1

*Drinky, drinky in a bar
Why, oh, why are you so far...
Up above the shelf so bright
A shining spirit in the night
Drinky, drinky in a bar
Why, oh, why are you so far...*

Reasons You Love Your Kids
#7

When they call for you to help them out, not your partner. That's a good feeling AND it makes your heart sink, if only because it means you have to stand up.

Top Ten Lies You Tell Your Children

#5

Bananas make your
poo yellow.
Apples make your poo green.
Kiwis make your poo hairy.

One Day You'll Thank Me:
Parental Advice
#7

Start your children watching – and
enjoying – your favourite TV shows
from an early age. Involve them in the
stories and the characters.
That way you'll never feel bad
about not watching any of their
programmes.

#5 Playlist
Scary Songs

Are your children screaming too loud? Are your kids fighting with one another? Do you want to drown out their incessant voices? Press play...

1. "War Pigs" – Black Sabbath
2. "Helter Skelter" – The Beatles
3. "Immigrant Song" – Led Zeppelin
4. "Symphony of Destruction" – Megadeth
5. "Cemetery Gates" – Pantera
6. "Angel of Death" – Slayer
7. "Seek and Destroy" – Metallica
8. "Ace of Spades" – Motorhead
9. "Caught in a Mosh" – Anthrax
10. "Wait and Bleed" – Slipknot

Shit Baby Name

#5

Nevaeh.*

*Judging by online trolls, you should never call your baby this no matter how religious you are.

Shit Baby Name Trend

#4

Pairing Colours and Nouns

A current baby naming trend is pairing nouns with colours. Why not match your favourite together when you name your next child. Let's get you started...

COLOUR	NOUN
Azure	*Lion*
Ivory	*Wolf*
Teal	*Bear*
Silver	*Cat*
Navy Blue	*Slippers*

COLOUR	NOUN
Pea green	Teacher
Grey	Love
Orange	Envy
Maroon	Car
Charcoal	Book
Aquamarine	Phone
Coral	Truck
Fuchsia	Glass
Wheat	Lamp
Lime	Bag
Crimson	Table
Khaki	Trousers
Hot pink	Garbage
Magenta	Pole
Plum	Piano
Olive	Tree
Cyan	Deer

66

If you have never been hated by your child, you've never been a parent.

99

Bette Davis

You Know You're a Parent When

#4

You consider a sleeping baby a higher high than any Happy Hour, sex or drug-induced wild night out you've ever had.

Bedside Companion

Are you in bed at 7.30 p.m.? Don't worry, you'll be awake at 3 a.m. with a newborn baby you're too terrified to put down in case it wakes up. These completely useless facts will keep you company.

1. In *The Empire Strikes Back* there is a potato hidden in the asteroid field.

2. Walt Disney suffered from musophobia – a fear of mice.

3. The pupils of a goat's eyes are square.

4. The word "Checkmate" in chess comes from the Persian phrase "Shah Mat," which means "the king is dead,".

5. To "testify" in court originated in Roman courts, where prosecutors and defendants swore on their testicles that they were telling the truth.

6. Underground is the only word in the English language that begins and ends with the letters *und*.

"

Raising kids is part joy and
part guerrilla warfare.

"

Ed Asner

Reasons You Love Your Kids
#8

Because they want to name the pet cat "Paul" or "Dinosaur" or "Lamp" or something equally ridiculous.

Tip-Top Tip
#1

Convince your children that
you have got them a cat,
but say that it likes to hide and
sleep. That'll buy you at
least 30 minutes.

Shit Baby Names #6

These names go without saying, right?

Adolf	Myra
Idi	Ted
Saddam	Jeffrey
Rudolf	Fred / Rose
Osama	Pablo
Genghis	Bernie
Pol	Lee Harvey
Mao	Leon
Josef	Benito

66

If evolution works, how come mothers have only two hands?

Milton Berle

99

Dad Jokes
#5

Q: What's the difference between in-laws and outlaws?

A: *Outlaws are wanted.*

You Know You're a Parent When #5

You buy slippers. Not because you're elderly, but because all manner of things could stab you from the floor.

CHAPTER
SIX

CREATURES
GREAT AND
SMALL

Icons of Parenting
#4

All Hail: Cersei Lannister

"The more people you love, the weaker you are. You'll do things for them that you know you shouldn't do. You'll act the fool to make them happy, to keep them safe. Love no one but your children; on that front a mother has no choice."

Cersei Lannister,
Game of Thrones, George R. R. Martin

Cersei Lannister is probably the strongest and strangest mother depicted on TV in decades. The first queen of Westeros, who sought to rule on the iron throne, was also the incestuous lover of her brother, Jamie, as well as the mother to his four children. Throughout the show, her character is defined by her complex (mis)understanding of motherhood.

She is a devoted mother, with unconditional love, and yet utterly ruthless. You always got the impression she'd throw any one of her kids under a bus if they ever got in her way or disobeyed her. And there's certainly no denying that they all ended up dead.

Guess What

#3

Children's soft toys and teddies – you know, the things they cuddle through the night, every night – have more than 2,549 germs per 100cm^2 – more than a toilet seat.

As seen on parent24.com

Reasons You Love Your Kids #9

Because they eat chocolate really, really, really slowly since they know it's a treat they might not get again for some time.

Tip-Top Tip #2

Buy a pillow with the face of your child printed on. Stuff the pillow into your face and scream loudly when you feel the urge arises. You'll feel better.

Shit Baby Names
#7

Kit.*

*Wayne and Coleen Rooney's latest signing.
(Surely not as in football kit?)

"

Having one child makes you a parent. Having two kids makes you a referee.

"

David Frost

Mum Joke

My daughter asked me what it's like to have children so I interrupted her every 10 seconds until she cried.

You Know You're a Parent When

#6

You pray brown smears on the sofa are just chocolate but decide to lick and smell it anyway to make sure.

We spend the first 12 months of our children's lives teaching them to walk and talk and the next 12 telling them to sit down and shut up.

Phyllis Diller

Shit Baby Name Trend

#5
Places

A ever growing celebrity trend is to name your child after the place they were conceived, or a location special to the parents' hearts. This is not quite so romantic for us non-famous plebs.

CELEBRITY BABY LOCATIONS	NORMAL BABY LOCATIONS
Brooklyn	Yaris (back seat)
Chicago	Shower
Zuma	Dagenham
Moroccan	Behind Lidl
Egypt	Premier Inn
Bronx	Slough
Tennessee	Chieveley Services (car park)
Milan	That Uber That One Time
Kingston	Honeymoon

Reasons You Love Your Kids
#10

When they give you a kiss
and a hug.
Because they want something.

(You taught them well).

Signs that Your Child is a Psychopath

You won't get this information in any other baby book, but we feel it's probably the information you, as parents, want to find out most. And first. Does this sound like your baby?

1. Superficial charm?
2. Inflated sense of self-worth?
3. Prone to boredom and requires vigorous stimulation?
4. Lies a lot?
5. Cunning and manipulative?
6. Shows no signs of remorse or guilt?
7. Demonstrates a lack of emotional range and empathy?
8. Impulsive?
9. Fails to take responsibility for any actions?
10. Lacks long-term goals?
11. Unable to control behaviours?
12. Copies the actions and behaviours of others?
13. Eats ice cream with fingers?

BaBy Talk
#2

Scientists believe that the origin of shaking the head to mean "no" actually derives from newborns turning their head away from food when they are full. Remember that next time you tell you kids no – you get it from them.

Alternative Nursery Rhymes #2

The bills for the house go up not down
Up not down, up not down
The bills for the house go up not down
All day long

Mummy of the house goes nag nag nag,
Nag nag nag
Mummy of the house goes nag nag nag,
All day long

*The daddy of the house goes @!***

Baby Talk
#3

Your baby will destroy
approximately 2,700 diapers
in the first three years
of its life.

Reasons You Love Your Kids #11

When they deliberately try to push your buttons to see how mad you'll get, you can't help but respect their disobedience.

Tip-Top Tip

#3

Never tell your partner that you had a good night's sleep. It'll be used against you later in the day when they want to get out of putting the kids to bed.

Cocktail Recipes
#3

Why not try one of our
signature cocktail recipes,
tailor-made for your
parenting moods...

#3: Rush Hour

Following a hectic day at work, your baby now needs play time, feeding and quiet time before their bath and bedtime routine. Give yourself a jolt of energy for the last lap of the day.

- Sugar
- Two shots of gin
- Half a can of quality imported beer
- Half a can of lemonade
- Squeeze of lemon and lime
- Shot of Jägermeister
- Extra virgin olive oil

Line the rim of your glass with sugar and drown two shots of gin with half a can of beer and half a can of lemonade. Squeeze in the lemon and lime and add the shot of Jägermeister. To grease the sides on the way down, glug in a good amount of extra virgin olive oil.

Shit Baby Names #8

Cash.*

*The son of Guns N' Roses guitarist –
drum roll, please – Slash.

" I used to believe my father about everything but then I had children myself and now I see how much stuff you make up just to keep yourself from going crazy. "

Brian Andreas

Pretentious Parenting Platitudes
#2

Even more parenting platitudes by people who think they know more than you.

"It is not what you do for your children but what you have taught them to do for themselves that will make them successful human beings."
   Ann Landers

"If you want children to keep their feet on the ground, put some responsibility on their shoulders."
   Abigail Van Buren

"Children have more need of models than of critics."
   Carolyn Coats

"*If you want your children to improve, let them overhear the nice things you say about them to others.*"
   Haim Ginott

"*I think that the best thing we can do for our children is to allow them to do things for themselves, allow them to be strong, allow them to experience life on their own terms, allow them to take the subway... let them be better people, let them believe more in themselves.*"
   C. JoyBell C.

"**When you teach your son, you teach your son's son.**"
   The Talmud

"**Parents often talk about the younger generation as if they didn't have anything to do with it.**"
Haim Ginott

"**What's done to children, they will do to society.**"
Karl Menninger

As seen on purposefairy.com

Games to "Play" with your Children

Have you ever noticed how many of the games parents have devised to play with their children usually involve the children running away and hiding from their parents. Here's the eight best games to "play" with your children when you need a bit of me time. OK, we've made some of them up...

1. The Quiet Game – who can stay quietest for as long as possible?

2. Hide and Seek – who can remain hidden for as long as possible?

3. Freeze! – who can remain still for as long as possible?

4. Treasure Hunt – who can remain distracted on a meaningless quest for as long as possible?

5. Sock Toss – who can help put away the laundry the quickest (before realizing they're completing a chore)?

6. Backwards Obstacle Course – who can pick up the obstacles already left on the floor the quickest and put them away where they belong (before realizing they're completing a chore)?

7. The Listening Game – who can sit and listen to Mummy/Daddy's TV show the longest? The person who writes down the most words wins!

8. Odd Drawer Out – who can sort and tidy the drawer with all the knick-knacks in it the quickest?

Guess What
#4

Today, in the UK, the estimated cost of a two-parent family raising a child up to the age of 18 is £150,783.

Reasons You Love Your Kids
#12

When they knowingly wipe their filthy and sticky hands on you, or make a mess, or smash things, because they know deeply, and without any doubt, that you're their slave, and you'll clean it up.

#6 Playlist
Stress Relief Songs

Tough day? Of course it was. But, let's be honest, you're not going to the gym to work off your stress, are you? So, instead, sit down, grab a pint of wine and let your mind slip away to these tunes, reported by a Mindlab study to be the world's most relaxing songs.

The tempo of each track matches the optimal resting heart rate of 60 to 65 beats per minute and the mid-range frequencies and absence of a low, heavy bass allow your nervous system to unwind.

1. "Weightless" – Marconi Union
2. "Electra" – Airstream
3. "Watermark" – Enya
4. "Mellomaniac" – DJ Shah
5. "Strawberry Swing" – Coldplay
6. "Please Don't Go" – Barcelona
7. "Pure Shores" – All Saints
8. "Someone Like You" – Adele
9. "Canzonetta Sull'aria" – Mozart
10. "We Can Fly" – Cafe Del Mar

Reasons You Love Your Kids #13

They try to delay going to bed –
by just a few more seconds – by
insisting that they
need to take another shit.

One Day You'll Thank Me:
Parental Advice
#8

If you give your child names with the initials A or B, they're more likely to achieve those grades at school. The same is true for stupid children with C, D and E for their initials.

The first half of our lives
is ruined by our parents
and the second half by our
children.

Clarence Day

You Know You're a Parent When

#7

You get upset that your child loves everything — their bike, YouTube, eating crayons — but can't say anything but "eugh" when you tell them you love them.

PreTenTious Parenting PlaTiTudes

#3

"Life affords no greater responsibility, no greater privilege, than the raising of the next generation."
  C. Everett Koop

"Your kids require you most of all to love them for who they are, not to spend your whole time trying to correct them."
  Bill Ayers

"There is no such thing as a perfect parent so just be a real one."
    Sue Atkins

"Most things are good, and they are the strongest things, but there are evil things too, and you are not doing a child a favor by trying to shield him from reality. The important thing is to teach a child that good can always triumph over evil."
    Walt Disney

"Parenting is not about having children lean on you but making leaning unnecessary. They have a compass, let them follow their own compass; freeing you up to be your own person on your own time and allowing them to become who they are to become."
    Wayne Dyer

Parenting Survival Kit:
Checklist

In order to survive this crazy little thing called parenting life, you'll need the following in order to be well and truly prepared. Without these items, collected in the order below, you'll be just as ill-equipped as any another parent. So, find them, the future of your child depends on it...

1. A lock of hair from a bald person.

2. An insurance policy without small print or hidden terms and condition.

3. A five leaf clover (golden, not green).

4. The name of a Wi-Fi provider that delivers on their promises.

5. The tip of a unicorn's horn.

6. A gym membership that is actually used to its full cost.

7. Three squirts of a bull's teat.

One Day You'll Thank Me:
Parental Advice
#9

When your child asks "Why?" to everything just reply, "It's magic!"

They'll believe magic exists and also shut up.

Father's Figures

#4

A parent checks their iPhone
to see what fun other
people are having, on average,
80 times a day.

> **"** Few things are more satisfying than seeing your own children have teenagers of their own. **"**

Doug Larson

One Day You'll Thank Me:
Parental Advice
#10

When your toddler starts
throwing a tantrum about
nothing, start laughing loudly.
Let them know that you're too
much of a wild card to
be reasoned with.

" Everybody knows how to raise children, except the people who have them. "

P. J. O'Rourke

How To Keep a Child Happy

Answers should be sent
on a postcard to the author,
Malcolm Croft,
c/o Welbeck Publishers.

Thanks.